God is

Wise

God is Wise

A children's book produced by
The Bible Tells Me So Press

Copyright © 2019
The Bible Tells Me So Corporation

PUBLISHED BY
THE BIBLE TELLS ME SO CORPORATION
2111 W. CRESCENT AVE, SUITE C, ANAHEIM, CA 92801
WWW.THEBIBLETELLSMESO.COM

First Printing July, 2019

God's much more
than smart.

Our God, He is wise.

His wisdom is seen
before our own eyes.

When we view the earth

and how it was made,

we easily see

God's wisdom displayed.

The clouds that float by,

thick, puffy, and round,

deliver water

that
falls
to
the
ground.

The dandelion

has seeds
that take flight;

the wind takes them to

**good
soil
and
light.**

Our God, He is wise.

He's so wise
indeed.

He knows everything

**and knows
what we need.**

God's wisdom is seen
in all that we view,

but mostly
it's seen...

in how He made you.

Jehovah by wisdom
founded the earth;
He established the heavens
by understanding.

Proverbs 3:19

For more
books, videos, songs, and crafts
visit us online at
TheBibleTellsMeSo.com

Standing on the Bible **and** growing!

Manufactured by Amazon.ca
Bolton, ON